The Huggabears

We the U.S.A.!

Tale 6

By Angelique La Fon-Cox

In every Huggabear storybook there is a hidden Huggabear Heart.
This book has 4! Hunt for them while you read!

Printed in the United States of America

Be sure to read ALL of the tales of
"The Huggabears"
And watch for NEW books yet to come!
www.thehuggabears.com

Tale 1	"Welcome to the Bearwood Forest!"
Tale 2	"Heavenly Castles"
Tale 3	"A Cold and Rainy, Wind-Whirly Day"
Tale 4	"The Family Gift"
Tale 5	"Promises of the Forest Berry Fairies"
Tale 6	"We Love the U.S.A.!"
Tale 7	"The Great Dinosaur Discovery"
Tale 8	"Flowers of the Meadow"

Dedicated to "Poppa" Frank Scopa
A Precious Friend and
Pearl Harbor Survivor

Also in memory of Walter and Ralph Conrad,
Brothers who went down with the USS Arizona during
the attack at Pearl Harbor

And
for all of the patriotic men and women of our great
nation who have contributed so much for the
freedom we enjoy today. God Bless you!

God Bless AMERICA!

It was another bright, beautiful and sunshiny day in the Bearwood Forest. Summer had come, bringing with it the warmth of the sun during the day, the glow of the fireflies in the evening and the song of the crickets throughout the night.

As on most days, the lovely white cottage was a buzzin' with busyness. Today was a very special day, it was the Fourth of July, one of the Huggabear Family's favorite holidays!

While Mommy bear was busy inside preparing the food for a wonderful patriotic picnic and Kooshla and Saboo were outside romping around in the forest, Daddy bear took little Tanuuk outside to decorate the lovely white cottage made of stone.

"Kooshla! Saboo!" Daddy bear called the little cubs, "Would you like to help us decorate the cottage?"

Kooshla and Saboo came scampering over to help Daddy and Tanuuk because they loved decorating for any occasion.

"What can we do Daddy?" Saboo asked eagerly.

"Would you like to help me put up our flag?" Daddy bear asked.

"Oh, yes!" Kooshla exclaimed, jumping up to grab the flag, causing it to almost drop out of Daddy bear's paws.

"Be careful my little one," Daddy bear said, "It is important that we do not let the flag touch the ground."

The puzzled little cubs looked up at him curiously.

"Why not Daddy?" Kooshla asked.

Daddy bear looked down at this little cubs.

"Our flag is a very important symbol of our nation. When others see the flag they know that it represents our great country. The colors of the flag are red, white and blue, and each color stands for different things.

"The red stands for bravery, the white stands for purity and the blue stands for justice. The stripes of the flag represent the 13 colonies from when our nation first began and the 50 stars represent the 50 states of the United States of *Abearica!*"

"Bearwood U.S.A!" the cubs cheered.

"That's right! And we have a special name for our flag too," Daddy bear said.

"Our flag has a name?" Saboo asked.

"Yes, it is known as *Old Glory*. It is also called *The Star Spangled Banner*," Daddy bear said.

"Like the song!" Kooshla shouted.

"Yes, that is what the song is about; our beautiful flag," Daddy bear answered.

We must always show our flag the proper respect it deserves. Special instructions called *The Flag Code* were written to teach how you should raise the flag, fly the flag, take it down and fold it.

Some of these rules are to never allow it to touch the ground, to keep it clean, not let it get torn and when it is flown at night to make sure it is properly lit and not leave it raised while in the dark. We do these things to honor our flag because it represents our nation, our freedom and those who fought to give us the gift of being free.

Kooshla and Saboo stood quietly listening and learning from their daddy about how to show proper respect for the flag.

Saboo pondered a moment and then asked, "Daddy, what is freedom?"

Daddy bear stopped what he was doing and sat down with his little cubs. "Freedom means that we can make our own choices for our lives. We can worship God Jehovah and His only Son Jesus without getting into any trouble. We can go to school and study the things we want to learn. We can find a job doing the work that we like to do. We can live where we want to live, go where we want to go, say what we want to say and enjoy all the blessings of life.

"Years ago, the settlers who came to this country wanted to live in freedom. There were many brave souls who made the choice to fight for that freedom so that in years to come, all who lived here, like you and me, could live in a country that was free. We need to appreciate that gift of freedom and be grateful for it.

"There are many countries in the world that are not free. It is important that we remember to celebrate our freedom and honor those who fought so bravely to give us that gift.

"Who gave us the gift of freedom?" Kooshla asked Daddy bear.

"Our freedom came from the brave heroes of our nation's past and present. We call them Veterans. There have been many wars during our nation's history. Some who fought in those wars lived and some died. They gave their lives to provide us with freedom. We must always show love and respect to everyone, but we must give special honor and respect to our Veterans. Without them and their service to our nation, we would not have the gift of freedom and live the lives we do today.

"We must also pray for our country each day and put God first in everything we do so He is able to guide and bless us. The Bible tells us in Deuteronomy 28:1 *"If you listen to the voice of God and obey His commandments, God will place you on high, high above all the nations of the earth."*

Just then Mommy bear came outside, "How is the decorating coming along?" she asked.

"Actually, we haven't even started yet!" Kooshla giggled.

"We have been learning important things to appreciate and respect in our country, like our flag, our Veterans—"

"And our freedom!" Saboo added with a smile.

"Oh how wonderful! Well, let me help you!" Mommy said as she picked up a blue star.

"It is important to know the history of our nation's past and remember the lessons learned to help us live better lives in the future," she said.

"What else should we know Mommy?" Saboo asked.

"We should know about our great leaders that did important works for our country, like Presidents *George Pawington*, *Thomas Bearfferson*, *Abearham Lincoln* and *Teddy Roosevelt*, just to name a few," she replied.

"They are the four Presidents of the *Mount Bearmore* monument in the state of *South DaKoala*," Daddy bear added, "My favorite monument is *The Statue of Libearty* in New York Harbor."

"Oh yes," Mommy bear sighed, "I will never forget the first time I saw her; such a magnificent sight to see. The *Statue of Libearty* was placed in the harbor to welcome all those who come to our great nation. Whenever critters see her they know she represents the place where dreams can come true; a place of freedom with hope for all," she finished with a smile.

"I believe it is important to keep the spirit of our nation alive in our hearts by teaching the history of our nation, honoring our Veterans and helping those in need. We must all keep the love for our country strong, appreciate our freedom and celebrate the Fourth of July, which is the birthday of our great nation!" Daddy bear said.

As the family decorated the lovely white cottage made of stone, they talked about all of the different things that made their country so wonderful. Soon the cottage was finished.

"Oh Mommy!" Saboo exclaimed, "The cottage looks so beautiful!"

"Yes!" Kooshla added, "I wish we could always keep it this way!"

"But there is still one thing missing," Daddy bear said.

"Old Glory!" Kooshla shouted. "Our grand old flag!" Saboo exclaimed.

Suddenly they heard some familiar voices coming up the winding dirt road. Uncle Mo Mo, Aunt Tinka, Koba and Mum bear had all come to have a patriotic picnic and enjoy the Fourth of July fireworks from the town of Bearford Falls. Everyone agreed the lovely white cottage looked very grand!

"You're just in time!" Daddy bear said greeting the family happily, "I was just about to raise the flag!"

Uncle Mo Mo helped Daddy bear raise the flag as the family stood silently, respectfully watching. As they did, Kooshla and Saboo thought upon all they had learned that day about their great country, their flag and their freedom.

When the flag had been raised, Mommy bear began softly singing the National Anthem. As she sang, the other family members all faced the flag, placed their right paws over their hearts and joined in singing with her loud and strong.

After they sang, they all recited The Pledge of Allegiance. Kooshla and Saboo's little hearts swelled with pride, for they really understood how blessed they were to live in such a great nation.

Cola

When they were finished the family members all clapped and cheered, for they too understood what a wonderful country they lived in and were happy to celebrate it.

Mommy bear then invited everyone to the back yard for a marvelous patriotic picnic. There was barbeque chicken, roasted corn on the cob with melted butter, Mum's perfectly pickled potato salad, warm baked bread, fresh fruit and sliced watermelon, strawberry cheesecake and freshly baked apple pie with homemade ice cream for dessert. To drink Mommy bear made forest berry juice and had ice cold Cubby Cola.

"Thank you Lord for this food," Kooshla and Saboo prayed, "Amen! Praise Jesus!" the cubs praised, waving their little paws in the air. It was an excellent Fourth of July celebration feast!

After dinner, all the cubs played games of croquet, Hide and Bear Seek and Bear Paw Ball with Daddy, Uncle Mo Mo until the sun went down and at last it was time for the fireworks to begin!

The family fathered together and watched the beautiful brightly colored fireworks as they exploded into the air surrounding Mount Bearford with their splendor and glistened across the sky.

It had been a remarkable day, one that Kooshla and Saboo would never forget. Now that they truly understood how blessed they were to live in such a place and would always show love, honor and respect for the great nation of Bearwood U.S.A., the United States of A*bearica*!

Mommy and Daddy bear gave Kooshla, Saboo and Koba each a bright and dazzling sparkler to hold. The excited little cubs were filled with joy!

"God bless *Abearica*!" Koba shouted.

"Happy Birthday to our great nation!" Saboo declared.

"We love the U.S.A.!" Kooshla exclaimed.

Mommy bear, Daddy bear and the rest of the family cheered with pride, happily joining the cubs in their celebration for they know that little ones only stay little for a little while.

The End

OPERATION HUGGABEARS

★ TEDDY BEARS ON A MISSION! ★

The OPERATION HUGGABEARS ministry is a project of The Huggabear Children's Project, Inc.

The idea for OPERATION HUGGABEARS actually came from HCP founder Angelique La Fon-Cox's then five year old daughter Aven. Aven wanted to know more about the war, the soldiers and their children. When her mother explained everything to her, Aven was greatly concerned for these children and wanted to do something speical for them personally. She told her mother they needed to send the children one of their cuddly Huggabears so the children could, as she said, "Have something to hug when they miss their mommies and daddies so much."

Moved by their daughter's thought and love, Josh and Angelique went to work immediately to begin the project. The soldiers are able to send their requests for a free Huggabear via email directly to Aven's email address. Once the request is received the bears are packed up and shipped out. Needless to say, we have had hundreds of happy children who receive a package with their beautiful, cuddly little Huggabear.

Aven works very hard going to radio stations, traveling to different Arizona cities and doing all she can to promote her project. She talks to people about sponsoring a Huggabear for a child of an American Soldier to show their support. The sponsors make a tax deductible donation of $20 for a bear package. This package includes one plush and cuddly Huggabear, an American flag with stand, an American hand book of history (donated by the Woodmen of the World Lodge #116). The donation also pays for the shipping and packaging and includes a personal sponsor gift card. With this gift card, the sponsor not only has the opportunity to write a direct message of support to the solider whose child will receive the bear, but they also have the opportunity to make an exchange of email addresses with that solider. This enables them to keep in touch on a regular basis one on one and become a prayer partner with an American Soldier.

If you would like more information on this ministry project or if you would like to sponsor a Huggabear for the child of one of our American Soldiers please feel free to contact HCP Inc. by visiting www.huggabears.org

Thank you and God bless America!

Special Thanks to...

My husband Josh Cox for giving of his time and brilliant talents in building to help create the sets for this book.

Heike Buchner for creating the beautiful Huggabear Family! I am so grateful to you for using your talents to help make this dream a reality! www.sunshine-teddies.com

My babies, Aven, MaCaedyn and Samuel Braden giving me such wonderful stories to tell and always being so happy to help me create new books. I love you with all my heart!

To John and Gerry Dillingham for all of your constant love and support of this ministry. God bless you both!

For MORE Huggabear books please visit: www.thehuggabears.com
Thank you for reading!

Dear Huggabear Friend,
Thank you so much for reading this story of *"The Huggabears"*, we hope that you enjoyed this one and that you will also enjoy our other books now available and coming soon. We also want to thank you for making a contribution to *The Huggabear Children's Project, Inc.*

The Huggabear Children's Project, Inc or *HCP Inc.* is a 501c3 Nonprofit organization founded and directed by Angelique La Fon-Cox and operated by the La Fon-Cox family as an extended ministry of the *"The Huggabears"* Christian children's book series. The ministry of HCP focuses on assisting children in need worldwide. With each purchase of a Huggabear product, a contribution is made to this fund.

It is our desire to gently plant seeds of the love of Jesus Christ in the hearts of children and share with them scriptures from the Bible, God's Holy Word. Through our stories and our work through *HCP*, we hope to provide positive influences for children and let them know they are loved, beautiful, important and special! We hope to speak for those who have no voice, help those who cannot help themselves and bring joy and the message of hope to those who are suffering. In doing so, we hope to make a difference in the world we live in through loving children, for when a child is loved it changes their lives and their future.

Please visit our website at: *www.huggabears.org* and visit our Facebook page at: *www.facebook.com/huggabears* to learn more about the projects of *HCP Inc.* and how you can get involved!
For Angelique's novel series *"The Intercessors"* please visit www.theintercessors.org
Portions of all book profits go to support HCP Inc.
God bless you and thank you again for reading our stories!

When you love a child, you change the world!
Angelique La Fon-Cox

45104622R00023

Made in the USA
Charleston, SC
10 August 2015